How Many Miles to Babylon?

Anne Elezabeth Pluto

LILY POETRY REVIEW BOOKS

For Zofia

I pulled into Nazareth, was feeling half past dead.

Robbie Robertson – "The Weight"

Table of Contents

Blessings

I have been blessed
with a violent childhood
with the pain of curses
thrown up as if to God
in language I understood
from the womb onwards.

I have been blessed
with survival skills
honed deep in the bone
dark twilight of remembrance
a city sewer surge of ugly
smells and complication

I have been blessed
and touched by human
hands and learned by rote
how best to escape the on-coming
darkness and not obey but
live to tell the tale best

By saying nothing at all -
To see, to feel, to flee -
The wounds do heal
and second sight the price
of this terrible reveal.

In the Beginning

There is only one
photograph of your mother.
She is an old woman with glasses
in a flowered dress,
headscarf, and high boots
holding a small child. A Russian cousin.

Far away in the thrice tenth kingdom
of the thrice nine lands your father
returned from the war that was meant
to end ALL war. You are four years old,
your mother is wearing a flowered dress,
a headscarf, high boots, and a sheepskin coat
she presents you as a gift
from the magi – he reaches to
embrace his young and beautiful wife – remembering
her long blonde hair – the warmth of her love -
you hit him – she is yours.

War-weary, hungry, he is not healthy
to understand this bond
and the gulf between you opens
a poem, a fissure, a blacksmith's hammer
in your small tight village.

My Father's Hands

Played with fire
Played with irons
Played with shoes
That horses wore
Proudly on hard packed
Dirt roads that led to the Border

My father's hands
Played with girls
Played with guns
Went to war

My father's tethered hands
Dug the airstrip trenches
Survived the Russian
Winter marches
And sleeping in the
Silent Soviet snow

My father's hands
Survived the famine
In the East
Survived the madman
Hiding in the Kremlin

My father's hands,
Held the rail of the boat
That crossed the Caspian Sea
Fed the orphaned bear
And learned to drive
Amidst the oil fields in Kirkuk
Where the prophet Daniel
lies my father's hands
Touched the Wall

The stones
The Sepulcher
The pyramids
The valley of the tombs
of kings
The graves of orphans
And things friends left
Behind my father's
Hand held my mother's
Wedding ring and long black hair
Held my newborn self
And breathed me pure into the winter air.

Post-Christmas Brooklyn Musings

I cannot see you - but I would
know you - long black hair
in a French twist red clip-
on earrings and your leopard
scarf. The murky shadows play tricks on me -
a winter mirage through the loaming
twilight in the barbershop window men
sit in chairs where nothing
has changed in 40 years. I want
to ask if they remember daddy -
didn't you go there to announce he wasn't coming
back? Your back is always to me
now: never your face:
your slightly lazy left eye that my
child inherited: winter retreats in the overheated
grocery store where the loose tea is
$19.95 a pound and not worth the price
I choose the next street
Back - past the school where I posed
for photos to send to the Soviet Union -
na pamets - to the grandparents - the little American
girl is starting school this year - wearing red
and black - your colors - the dark comes quickly now passing
the large one and two family homes - Christmas
lights open a hole into the evening
the B train has stopped on its way to the sea.
I meet the other winter people on the corner where we cross Beverley
Road and separate. I look back for a moment something shuffles in
ghostly silence nearby. An animal?
Above the holiday lit houses the sky is cavernous and black.
I can never go home.

* *na pamets — Russian — for remembrance*

January Sonnet

The birds come back in pairs
to try the Christmas feeders
navigating the squirrel proof
plastic to catch the seeds in
their beaks – the snow recedes
until the next storm – dead leaves
wet and mulched glister in
the weak afternoon sun I never
want to leave - dreamt my dead self
the ghost in this yard – tossing a ball
to the dog – who chases it and brings
it back in shadows – substance recedes
and we will live forever unbroken
a January circle of omitted time.

Valentine

On my desk
the winter sun streams
through the third-floor windows.
You are there framed – twice.
Once
before we met
in another country
the sun in your eyes.
The second
after we had
found each other's heart
open and willing
you ride a bay horse
the prairie winds to the endless
horizon – your hair blown off your face
that looks away from the camera.

I've thrown the papers on the floor
in careless surrender – and step
around them – the clock hums on the wall
the music plays through me
the quiet room
my heart beating – 2000 miles west
between the photographs
the snow and ice come as if to baptize
the winter hours
short days to long nights.
You will come
East
to me, the journey
of a star already risen

the sun behind you —the horse tethered
the milky way ahead
the silver moon in my hair
throw a rope around the constellations
and bring it all to me.

On the day we got your diagnosis

The air feels like snow – but the storm
is inside the restaurant – quiet at 2:00
you are waiting for a burger and fries
in a booth at the back – neither of us will
cry in public. The nurse told you to tell
me – it is only fair – the last few weeks
heavy - punctuated by the cold - and your
need to turn up the heat. You keep yourself
busy – guitar – the trial – plans for the spring garden
that may never happen now.

Rings

You wear the wedding ring
on your middle finger – slipped there
as a placeholder and then stuck – spring
settling in and we are virus bound to each
other – the weather will only get warmer
and the ring, like a noose, will not loose
my father's was cut and left in the ivory
box from the Toronto jeweler – and there
was another – my mother's first husband.
I've sold two rings when the price of gold
was high – my fingers swell in summer and
the band hurts.

Chess

There is no playbook
for the dead.
The dying
The caretakers.
The family.

Hospice provides a map –
Drugs arrive delivered right
to the front door –
Nurses – chaplains – social workers
volunteers –
Contraptions – beds that breathe
Throughout the day and night -
oxygen that becomes a lullaby
sheets of paper to keep score:
Morphine – 4
Patient – 0
Haldol – 5
Patient – 0

Syringes filled to
the correct line – gently
insert in the inside
of his cheek.
That didn't hurt
until the end.

We play chess
the set that arrived
from Istanbul.
I always play for Salaheddin
you for Richard and
his Templars.
I walk you through

every move – I let you
win – and then
the Knights
the Pawns
the Queens
the Rooks
the Imams and Bishops
the King and Sultan
get put away.
I have not opened
them since that day – it hurts
to see them in
their splendor.

Morphine

I don't cry unless I hear the songs
I fought to play – my own
struggle and impatience – your
voice coming back over the caprock
prairie – all cattle lowing and cotton
blowing in thorny circles – the hawks
visible in the hot July sky – blue
until the end – your eyes were alive
even when you could only whisper
even when you called me by some
other woman's name – even when
you begged me to overdose you.
It's silent now
It's hot and all I can hear
are the birds.

Bird Dream

Tiny baby – with feathers and personality
in the palm of my hand – his face resting and
trusting – little things that fill up the heart –
how did I miss the eggs – how did I miss
the hamster who flattened out
and snuck into the cage – now in
the food watching me and filling
cheeks with millet.

As dreams go – this one remains – the birds
are always singing – not trusting me – yet
lose their appetite if a neighbor feeds them.
How little did I know
about love.

Hush puppy

I stop taking notes when hospice
arrives – and the notebook in my
purse becomes a scratch pad
for shopping lists – for restaurant
menus – Shakin' Seafood
does not have fried okra
no matter how many
times I ask
no red beans
no, we are not in Texas
but they do have a fried
Catfish basket with French
Fries, onion rings, and hush puppies.

the dog under the bed
listens to the undulating sound of
the mattress – your weight shifts in
the night of disturbed sleep – in the
beginning there is only the TV
that I turn off once you are
sound asleep –
Hush puppy.

Dog and Bed

Your death was easier
in winter – The Dog still
alive – my constant companion
learning to navigate the world
with only his right eye – I had
to bring myself completely to
the table – the one where
I hand fed him on the kitchen
floor disguising medications
to look and taste like treats.

He was brave – the cold January
afternoon when you died – he sat
next to me – suspended – the pewter
silence of the new year pressing
in my throat – the hospice nurse
came to fill out papers – and the funeral
director sent two young men –
they were late – it was a good day
for death – and we waited
warped in silence.

When they arrived – The Dog
walked to the fence to guide
them in patiently sitting by
the hospital bed as they
wrapped you in your sheet
lifted your washed and broken body
onto a gurney – the dog watched.
They zipped and once again he
led them out to the gate.

I turned off the bed – the mattress
deflating – the snake like hissing
at its unnatural end.
All is silence.
That night I still slept
on the couch – I had
forgotten how
to use a bed.

What You Left Behind

Your notebooks
where there are
messages I cannot bear
to open - you left
guitars and music fishing
line and reels – poles
and lures – flys on
the wall assemblages of
feather and white tailed
deer to fool the large mouth
Bass hooks and weights
your clothes – your Stetson hats
Lucchese boots – chaps –
I am separating
by size to divide no one
will play dice to receive
a chess set from Istanbul
a gift for me we played
the first few months of hospice
your focus shifting – I find notes
on how the Queen moves as far as
She can see in all directions – but how little
joy enjoys the Queen thereof – for I am
She and altogether joyless.

Into the Heart of the Dust

I'm finding you in books – open
the dust jacket revealed that
God is alive – you were always
a searcher – a believer – a
deceiver – you took notes
to remember what you read
God is love – and heaven
is a place where you wait
at the gate for Peter – the rock.
Roll away the stones – the
Gospels of prosperity – the
Pentecostal prairie pageant
you were born into – the Texas
wilderness – all tumbleweed
and rifles – cows and horses
second amendment – the well
guarded militia – the assault
rifles you carried as a Ranger.
It fades into the horizontal
the looming highway: North
to Amarillo – East to Dallas
South to El Paso – West
to New Mexico – I'm going
stand in the marketplace
at Clovis and buy a pair
of pointy boots – I'm going too
scatter the dirt of the earth
in memory of the dead
the maligned – the innocent
I'm going to sing my heart
into the heart of dust –
the carefully tended
acre of mistrust.

El Paso

I thought, perhaps you were here
the house so dark that even the dead
could find their way back – how is it
that you are gone – I tried to find the portal
the hole in the sky that would open
and you would rise from your broken body
and touch the gate – where those ponies
lost in childhood to terrible accidental deaths
were whole and grazing – lifting their
magnificent heads in wait – and you
a child in a big hat – broken-in boots and
silver spurs with jingle bobs that sing
and rake the pasture – the trail
you leave behind only a hole in the sky – the Wolf
Moon beckoning forward – the house silent
the dog finally at rest.
The winter
this winter
and you in that Texas pasture – tenderly resting your face
in the neck of your first pony –
the paint horse from El Paso.
Let everything be made holy
again.

Widow Poet

At the poetry reading
the widows line up to
tell me they understand -
one of them offers a hug
arms outstretched as far
as COVID allows – but only
one buys a book – the others
pass me as if at a wedding -
onto the receiving line
on to the three male poets
book in hand
for signature and purchase.

More things that I have lost

My childhood desk
My mother's gold earring in the Ditmas Junior High School gym
My first love
My best girlhood friend
My cat Ginger
My rabbit Honeysuckle
My mother's crucifix
My chance of having other children
My best college friend
My bass guitar
My first car
My silver hoop earrings (pairs # 7,8,9,10,11)
My box of love letters
My first pair of cowboy boots
My long dark hair
The last horse I rode.

October Requiem

For Anna Politkovskaya

A thousand souls
to see you
and carnations
their powdery scent
to fill the ugly space
and candles to light
the darkness – it is a congregation
of the astonished
those who knew you
and those who knew
your words.
Brave is hardly enough
to describe your actions.
You who have eaten the knowledge
of your death foretold.
You who have negotiated with gunmen
listened where no one else
dared to even speak
You who have written
what should not have been
acknowledged. You who have taken
the plight of the ordinary
conscript against his commanding
officer – You who have said *they are human*
too in Chechnya. And after all that
you loved your county
and its broken people
in the face of skewed
democracy. Anna, I live
in the land of the free
and the home of the brave
but we don't see the flag

draped coffins arrive – we don't
see the mother, the wife, the lover,
the father, the brother, the son, the daughter
waiting to take that body home,
denied our national grief – it's blood
for oil –God where he hardly belongs
divide and conquer – be still –
No one should die in vain.

When he came into the apartment
did you know
what did you feel
at that last moment
did you look at him
the hired assassin
and ask – *have you come to shoot me?*
or to fuck me?
It can be the same
word in Russian
Did you beg for mercy?
Did you call out to the Mother of God?
Or did you stand there
and whisper
I have long been expecting you.

I won't cover the mirrors
40 days you'll wander the earth
come settle here – as you should
never die – be spirit to us all
instill your fearless heart among us

who take for granted what is
our birthright
the simple thing
the freedom
of our speech.

*Anna Stepanovna Politkovskaya (née Mazepa; 30 August 1958 – 7 October 2006)
was a Russian journalist and human rights activist, who reported on political events
in Russia, in particular, the Second Chechen War (1999–2005). On 7 October
2006, she was murdered in the elevator of her block of apartments, an assassination
that attracted international attention. In June 2014, five men were sentenced to pris-
on for the murder, but it is still unclear who ordered or paid for the contract killing.*

Slava Bogu**

Red leather boots, embroidered blouses
Flower crowns and fairy tale houses –forest
deep with wolves and witches
snow sinks silent into holes
of foxes and rabbits – invaders from the East
kill the men – pick the women
one by one to ride and ride
and Ride
the fastest horses on earth can only
go so far – centuries later this is all
a mystery – and golden domes rise
to the defenders – our blood mixed
and hot – old wounds bound in stained
linen – brick red Easter eggs in crystal dishes
Defend the Defenders
Glory to the Defenders
Glory to the city
Glory to God in the Highest.

**Glory to God – Old Church Slavonic*

Saint Olga's Stained Linen

The Mongol hoards destroyed her tomb.
She was a woman – after all and not
worth the veneration of her memory.
She was a woman – in a brass crown
with covered hair – who watched
her husband pulled apart
by horses. No one should witness
a death so terrible the earth
soaked scarlet with blood. The widow
left to put his body back together.
She could not make him the Lord of the Dead.
She could not make him Christ to rise with dread.
She became the saint of defiance and vengeance
instead.

In My Church, Mary Wears Red

The Moscow Patriarch had repeatedly bestowed blessings on the Russian military, giving a historical golden icon of the Virgin Mary to a senior commander, for example, and casting the war as a holy struggle to protect Russia from what he called Western scourges like gay pride parades. He has been a vocal supporter of President Vladimir V. Putin, with the church receiving vast financial resources in return.

Neil MacFarquhar and Sophia Kishkovsky
New York Times April 18, 2022

Let's take Her out of the picture.
Out of the historical golden frame
where She wouldn't stand
for being in the pocket of a general
scourge – the cold eastern blame
of the west. She sees the exchange
of gold and gems – what those who
do not have eternal life see fit
to deal with – let's take Her out
of this picture - She's left on a train
to the sea - She's standing in the graves
found in Bucha - She's wandering in
the steel plant in Mariupol – this Holy
Week – this Passover feast – this month
of fasting – She's covering her hair – her face –
She's opening her hands and reading
the central list of the dead – She's
stepping into the *Chorne more* *
swimming mermaid like her red garments
trailing the fishes and every broken mother's
wishes to pull the dead sailors to shore
in militias – to show – to show - their weeping
mothers – their blinded criminal country the cost
of lies – the cost of lives – and She rises
Venus like from the sea – Stella Maris -

Theotokos** – Mother of Jesus – announcing
the resurrection in this, the cruelest month
of the year.

*Ukrainian: Чорне море, romanized: *Chorne more,*
 IPA: [ˈtʃɔrnɛ ˈmɔrɛ] Black Sea
** Greek: Mother of God

How many miles to Babylon?

Three score miles and ten.
Can I get there by candlelight?
Yes, and back again.
If your heels are nimble and your toes are light,
You may get there by candlelight.

How many miles to Babylon?
Three score miles and ten
Can I get there by candlelight?
Yes, and back again.

Back to black and Sarin gas
Back to the ancient deceptive past
How many miles to Babylon?
How many miles and then we'll be gone?

Back to dust and back to shame
Back to curse God's merciful name
How many miles to Babylon?
How many miles to cross the moon
Within a star – to show the world
We cannot really have come very far.

How many miles to Babylon?
To ride the backs of wolves and foxes
And carry guns – repeating rounds
That start with a click – a press
And then the dead – the living
Will undress – and throw them all
In an unmarked grave – the world
Is full of ghosts and we, their slaves.

How many miles to Babylon?
Three score miles and ten
Can I get there by candlelight?
Yes, and back again.

How the Nile was Made

When Isis was still Nu
the great mother -
She married her own
dead green brother and bore
his children - gave the world
the river – where she planted
her golden sandals and poured
water from a charmed jug -
walked on the backs of crocodiles
shut their gaping mouths with a soft
hand she rode side saddle on the back of a hippopotamus
into the sub-Saharan desert snaking the course
of the sacred river to the lake
where she returned - centuries later
to see Stanley meet Livingston
and she wandered on the banks – hiding in
the reeds when Moses was the baby in
the basket – she saw the royal procession
of sister wives emerge – strayed by the
tomb of golden Alexander and counted
the centuries of pilgrims at his hot and sandy mausoleum
she saw the last pharaoh of Egypt wear Her robes
and call for immortal longings holding river creatures
in her beautiful hands – death takes them all - the sacred
river runs past Adam and Eve's – past damage and thieves
past all she could have imagined or believed.

Isis

In broad daylight they snatched it,
that black-flag gang, the killers
and their web of sable-clad spiders
spying on neighbors in the name
of *the* God.

You slumber
In Nile ooze, flowing in linens,
in sandals of halcyon and lapis lazuli
you awaken dead scarabs; Cleopatra bore you
as her serpentine skin. You
cannot be killed: as they raise flags
to mask their visions you side-
saddle the hippopotamus

In your muddy underworld,
measure souls in hieroglyphs.
Let the rivers swallow them.
You will turn your painted eyes
as they hurtle before you, legions
ticking in suicide vests, hefted on spines
on severing heads – *no Kara koz*
virgins await you in this molten heaven;
you will unleash the peacock angel
and mothers and grandmothers' bone
shall be crushed into new flesh, new skin
at the resurrection of Sinjar,
their unearthly mass grave: horrors
horrors bleeding on your palate - the goddess
with the stolen name.

Funeral in Al-Malikiah 2019

In memory of Hevrin Khalaf

Hevrin,
Your name should be a place.
Heaven or Hebron

Should hold the martyred weight
of your memory,

should trace you
pulled from your car

head bashed and beaten
face and legs slashed

dragged by hair
torn from your head –

you free fall forward -
four shots to the back,

pronounced dead.
Hevrin.

Hevrin, you lived and died
for women's suffering in Raqqa

Only your jaw intact,
but mother still knows your face.

Oversized purple flowers and plastic doves
drape your bridal-red coffin in white lace.

mourners usher you to your final resting place.

Hevrin Khalaf (Kurdish: Hevrîn Xelef, Arabic: ہفرین خلف, also Khelef;
15 November 1984 – 12 October 2019) was a Kurdish-Syrian politician and civil
engineer. Khalaf served as the Secretary General of the Future Syria Party. She
was executed by Turkish-backed Ahrar al-Sharqiya fighters near the M4 Motorway
south of Tell Abyad during the 2019 Turkish offensive into north-eastern Syria,
on 12 October.

Cartel

Dove and aloe
palm and oleander
pretty poison
magenta bougainvillea
highway in the desert
hidden smell of silent
cattle straight miles
away the hot sun
comes upon us
sweat and blood
a fence that cannot
work – a war of equals
violent pursuit of cash -
the law of blood
and dismemberment
guards the border, and
life goes on
and on
and on.

\When I seek out the Damned

It's a long tunnel – something we crept
in as children – hunched over in our
make believe worlds of
Follow the Leader
Cops and Robbers -
Cowboy and Indians –
red light – green light
– one – two – three -
Let me count again – one gunman
and how many Texas law men
in the hallway
the rounds of the repeating AK 15
reverberate on CNN
the law men run backwards –
This isn't how it's supposed to be
a western movie – the guy with
the badge and big hat always
moves forward – even if he
doesn't win.

I shall wear a robe and crown

I've stopped believing
in the afterlife – this must
be Hell already – and the demons
have fistfuls of dollars
that never are enough.

I've stopped believing
that all men are created
equal – on paper – where
it matters once fertilization
has been accomplished.

I've stopped believing
that the stone can
roll away and there's
The Messenger in his
Risen state – look over
Jordan – take up your
robe and crown.

Take it up
and put it down.

Shakmati*

I don't want to remember, but I
feel the incidents move through
me like water – muddy, murky, silt
on the bottom – bodies locked
in death embraces – we were stupid
I take that back where it belongs, the
heart cannot be commanded, at times
artfully restrained, but not told how
and what and where to move, there
are moments, when the present pain,
the despair of trial and error evades
me – what I have shaped, with my hands
and time, what I have reinvested in
removes itself by circumstance, then I
go backwards and wish I had not
moved at all.

Chess – in Russian.

Contentious Love

You called us wolves
my husband and I
too beautiful
circling each other but missing
the scent – you were blunt
like a knife that no longer
cuts straight but
encompasses the skin like
a threat and enters unpredictable -
I must have missed the signs
a sky full of filmy stars and a waning
wet moon singeing the August
air – you were expecting
a girl and had picked out her
name but the signs were turned
towards the dirt where your faucet
dripped and tomatoes grew in perfect
red abundance - you brought them in
to the office – bragging on your bounty -
that was the last time I saw you – in
your kitchen where you made it clear -
the coffee was my exit door – my
regret filled the table separation
and divorce in my future – we
let go and never spoke again - the stars
align in asymmetrical perfection –

your mother died
today – complications
COVID – we met only
once – twenty years ago
in the house where you
grew up – and dreamed
of escape – the view from

a perfect picture kitchen window
the yard in the rain – trees
naked in the cold spring – a day
not unlike today - you posted her
engagement photo on Facebook to
admit how your contentious love
was eternal – and your flurry
of friends condolenced you in
the public viewing that will
serve for her wake
the dead and turn the clock
upside down upon its head.
The silence in your mind
will truly serve for dread.
I open my volchitsa* eyes and count
the stars.

*Russian for Female wolf.

Polite Excuse

I'm going to remember you, keep it short
and keep you in the moment where we
return to the resilient summer silence
the heat that came off the sidewalks in
waves – it was a long goodbye – you
never looked me in the eye or explained
the oncoming silence – that covered me
like snow – it's cold to lose a friend you love
to move through your heart in circles – to
learn to forget without swift regret that
what was left behind was not worth the time
or the kind words you would write years later
when I suggested the possibility of meeting for coffee
only to receive a polite excuse for an egress.

Girlhood Landscape

I remember your shoes
and that you were slightly
clubfooted – in your beautiful
sister's sky-blue patent leather
hand-me-downs – prancing towards school
with your straight dark hair waving
behind you – a banner to announce
your coming – we would meet
the next year in 2nd grade – in class
where nothing was ever equal between
us – there is much damage created
by status – I remember your parents
house – where your kind and unattractive
father saw his patients – that was before
the advent of prozac –
that was when people
talked – over dinner in the dining
room we could hear the beauty
fucking her boyfriend and your father
begging your drunk mother to go
upstairs and stop the noise.

I remember your twin
autistic broken brother
who ate his own shit and we
sang to him – you loved
him the most – having shared
your disastrous mother's womb
and emerged enlightened he will
always be your other.

There's a fly in the ointment
whenever we have attempted
to reconcile decades

of difference – plastic
surgery stretches your mouth
into a scimitar – a moon arc
a middle age parenthesis –
your tall sons chose
their father when the marriage
tottered – and your sister wrote
me and I reached out to you
again – why did I bother – you
gave me a lecture on my mother's
stroke – no fortune or good luck
there – I've passed you on the street
in the other direction – in my red tights
and black shoes – I'm going home
and that is my news.

Dramatic Transition from Independent Sources

For M

If I only knew how – this is
the simple story – not found
online – but in the small dark
corner of conversation
at a party – this one New Year's Day
among strangers you confess your family
origin – you were lost – given away
at birth – DNA has become the key
that unlocks every door – the policeman
on the floor – the mother forced to endure
birth and then turn her head in shame –
the baby taken still unnamed but in her
breath she remembered you until
death (do you part) the family now appears
without art – a dramatic transition from
Independent sources.

Conditional Tense

At best – if –
the clock could be unwound
the season spinning down
years of paper calendars –
making a ladies' fan of time
the memories would remain
intact – but – if – at best
the solid refrain when
we are sloppy in our cups –
I would beg the question –
feel the spring in my hair
listen to the train on its way
to the sea – and still you
would be there – a boy
in a green shirt – before
everything that happened
later and was written
in the dirt.

Gravesend

In the late autumn on a Friday
or Saturday night – we passed
the graves at Gravesend – quite
by accident – I am always drawn
to the dead and pulled you towards
the quiet leafy slate grey darkness
the toppled memorials that lay
buried for 300 years – to stand
among the unremembered
the vanished – Lady Deborah Moody
in a possible unmarked x marks
her spot – this treasure map
of bones – a woman found this
colony – in voluminous skirts and
court shoes she played the Dutch
and British too – I never played
you but for my buried hurt – my
slate heart which you broke
and broke again – the last words
remain. The most searing – the
un-endearing strain of first love
settling beneath the October light
under the neglected dead in Gravesend.

Deborah, Lady Moody (born Deborah Dunch) (1586– circa 1659) is notable as the founder of Gravesend, Brooklyn, and is the only woman known to have started a village in colonial America. She was the first known female landowner in the New World. As a wealthy titled woman, she had unusual influence in New Netherland, where she was respected. In the Massachusetts Bay Colony, where she had first settled after leaving England because of persecution as an Anabaptist, she had been described by contemporaries as "a dangerous woman" and chose excommunication over giving up her beliefs.

I wish Wisława Szymborska could edit my poems

We would meet in the space between
terror and delay – in a room lined
with books and drink tea from bone
china cups – she would pour over
my lines with the eye of a phoenix
and translate my meager imaginings
into the Mother tongue I cannot
yet speak - I would not answer
in my diminishing Russian vocabulary
parting the lace curtains and levitating
towards the East. I am moving backwards
with every book I read – and she is
there – solitary figure at the desk
cigarette smoke curing above her
head – waiting in the corridor
reserved only for the dead.

Good Friday 2018

The grey wet sky – color of dread
memories of your anger fill the space
and clench me to the desk – there was
nothing bright those years before
I could leave – nothing light – the color
of an open window looking
over the alley courtyard – the sky
appeared like Heaven – cumulonimbus
clouds hung in suspended animation
and I wished – no - I dreamed of opening the door
and leaving – coming into my own sense
of what home could mean – you were so bleak
a haunting apparition long before your death
at 92 – you circled the long hallway – the forever
L shape searching for my faults – making lists
that I repeat like prayers – for the resurrection.

Akhmatova in Paris with Modigliani

You had emigre status – a hole
through the fence – where the avenues
circled around the river – spring bloomed
in eternal resurrection – the cold – the war
the dead – the silver era left behind
for just a short time – you were courted
by artists – you lovely tall girl – your crow
black hair – he painted it blue in the portrait
blue in his hands blue in the bed – where everyone
could be forgotten, where death was as close
as breathing in the Paris spring through
the window – where you had tossed your
blue silk stockings on the chair
you chose not to remain. The motherland
was calling – the blood and souls would
need your words.
You left.
The hole in the fence repaired with iron.
And you never looked back.

We started out as liars

For MKS

You were a gentile
my family were Poles.

You were a Jew
and we are Russians.

For the most part
it is only a story

you tell to survive
a fiction that follows.

A chapter.
A mystery.

A test.
Then it is over.

And we rest.
We rest.

Mother to Remember

For MKS

Your yahrzeit will arrive
on the 20th of Av, 5780
Dog day August – 8th month – 10th day
the Magus twirling the yikzor flame into silver tracks
I haven't been back to Brooklyn since
before we knew the pandemic would
take us all under - that didn't kill
you fell on the emerald carpet staircase
hemorrhagic stroke
husband, housekeeper, doctor neighbor –
call 911 – sirens rush to Maimonides – you
never woke up - by the third day
it was decided – they came in pairs and said goodbye.
I wasn't there – joined the funeral by Zoom
reduced to the broken angry girl whose
life you saved in 11th grade – I didn't get
to say goodbye –no photograph remains
I saved your letters –
spider penmanship and blood maroon ink –
You were my favorite teacher –
who lived in my favorite house – on my favorite street
the subway stops recede on the BMT tracks
the silver train pulls out of the station this is
no longer home – all is memory and
distance – all is love and love and
love.

The Tricorne Hat Lady

My mother didn't give her up easily. She gave me the fisherman –
the Dutch girl bell and the Delft windmill salt and pepper shakers.
But the Tricorne Hat Lady came with me after my mother's stroke
– wrapped in newspaper and hidden in the boxes of jewelry that I
brought from Brooklyn to Boston on my first trip back.

I coveted her as a child. I wanted to be her – the made in Occupied
Japan figurine – her hat at a jaunty angle – blue and white as Delft
but with a hint of pink in her basket of flowers – always smiling – her
china hair a lighter shade of pale – almost silver as my own – her 18th
century peplum jacket and skirt – she is looking at someone – was
there a male companion – a Ross Poldark of sorts that was making her
laugh - someone that was lost or broken.

She lay in the box for 7 years – in the fallow field of a bedroom closet
– wrapped in history until this year when I found her again – my old
pretty friend – smiling and shiny blue – her skirt still in alignment
with her jacket – the flower basket on her hip – the hat always just
right - she sits on my desk amid the papers and books – the lists of
things I need to do – her ghostly face a doorway back to dreaming of
what could happen next.

No Exit

For Zofia

I take the wrong exit –
the one right
before the turn off
to the Fenway - we go
over the Mass Ave bridge
the twilight spreading through
us as this is not a path we have
ever travelled together – 21 years
we crossed the river – in a car – on a train –
you in your baby stroller when
the green house was burning through
the bright autumn and I avoided
Harvard Street to shield you from
the smoke – we turn onto Memorial
Drive and take the BU Bridge into
your childhood where I am the first
to note – *This stretch of Comm. Ave makes me sad.*
And you agree. The price of alteration
finds us riding the trolley tracks
into Allston – to the safety of loss
I am remembering how many
years I lived here – part of this fabric
never leaves – the house where you
were made – made over into luxury
I could not now afford – this edifice
of stability - we drive out to where
Twin Donut forks the road in neon
pink against the reprimanding sky
the road widens where the nuns
were smart to see the change and
change with it past the hospital
and into the Hassidic enclave
of tight brick and triple decker

streets of families and students
I drop you off – your first shared
apartment – you have just
waved goodbye to your partner
and now your mother – I pause
and see you disappear into
the dim hall light – a tall shadow
trailing up the stairs.

Bad Memories

Today I drive out
through the pine highway
that ultimately leads to the sea
it was this kind of weather – bright
with cloud cover that did hover in the silver
light of the train that came from
the heart of the awakening city.

It was not a journey worth remembering
retracing my path backwards driving
towards the scene – I haven't played
it forward – just shuffled it among
lost items – dead leads – forgotten
but for the present – how I came
here – how the lies were effervescent
and the trip home was clouded
there is always shame in these moments
a sad half smile at someone else's story
when it comes too close to the truth.

The Farm Road Forward

Connects me out of the neighborhood
past the hospital and the old police stables where now

all signs point to another medical facility – the horses
gone but the stable remains and the steers from the

farm reach over the fence to scratch their horns against
the bottle brush pines – always together – since

birth and protected forever – they call the winter birds with
soft bellows near the pond where they see their large reflection

Narcissus in treble softness – always a surprise – in the twilight
coming back from work – the deer caught me unaware and

I slow down - the road still while they stop and
watch – before turning white tails and jumping

the fence never looking back but prancing forward a disappearing
act into the verdant deep where the trees are thick and no

one lives. In the morning the coyote sit like dogs and survey
the cars – scratching their ears with hind legs – they are too

close to the road – the Canadian Geese plow the fallow autumn
fields in twos, in fours, in eights, and then alight while the turkeys

come and scatter. I see them in Brighton – near the Hamilton
Grammar school – walking on Chestnut Hill Ave as if they owned

it – at night as I break the recycle boxes – the raccoons
come out to watch and I speak to them as if they were my dog

each one more curious, one as big as Bulgakov's black cat devil
and the baby who wants to sit in my lap – their masked faces

a Halloween costume party in the yard – they climb the tree
and turn their polished eyes to see if I am still there – they

dance and turn in circles - disappear into the blue-black air.

Books

I have carried books with me since I was 18, thinking
nothing of packing them in boxes – moving them out of
one apartment and into another – stacking them in sacred
Geometry - too many now – and fight to figure librarian
calculus to position them on shelves that are not
generous – they each have meaning – aside
from the writer and the research – each one found
its way to me in precious servitude – a few carried
by my father – across 11 countries in the raging
Russian war wounded winter – I cannot phantom the
construct – the grammar of salvation – of deliverance
and the alphabet to transform books into purpose.

I have only you to blame – at 5 you took me
to the bookstore on the corner of Albemarle and Flatbush
near the movie theatre and let me pick out my first books
My forever friends – *A Children's Garden of Verse* – *Russian Fairy Tales* -
The Arabian Nights –
where I landed – and I carried
grammatic hope and the knowledge that women
are the ones who weave the remains of ruin
and watch the moon – the crescent scimitar
who keep the edge sharp
who decide to live to tell the story.

Grief

I find it in my hands
listen while tuning
the guitar – I'm always sharp
but that suits my voice – I find
the grief in the bookcase – pull
out volumes I could give
away – put out on the sidewalk
in boxes – it should be that easy
sometimes I just walk from room
to room – thinking I have forgotten
something – and then – as if
pulled back by shiny objects – akin
to the crows across the street
I settle and read – a chapter
a poem – a map to find
my way back home.

Christmas Weather

I'd like to write
and tell you all
that I remember
December – like today –
five years lost now
backwards – who could read
the weather – the entrails of
dead animals – a prediction
of future ire. Who could
certainly not you – not even
me. I'd like to
write and tell you
all that the forgotten do
remember – when love
dies – sex is not the memory
but the texture of the weather
the winter birds in red berry
bushes – the snowstorm –
the moments of sheer joy
and overarching loss.

All of this I toss
aside – I'd like to write
my heart out from inside.

Acknowledgements

This book could not have happened without the love, support, and generosity of others. First and foremost, Gloria Monaghan who suggested I attend the Lily on the Cove retreat and Manuscript clinic. That's where this collection truly began. Many rounds of applause to my splendid and multi-talented editors, Eileen Cleary and Christine Bess Jones, whose careful ear(s) and eye(s) to detail grew a manuscript into a book. Special thanks to my writing workshop partners in the Wild Geraniums and the Chive Collective. Thank you all for believing in me and in this book.

The following poems first appeared in the *Muddy River Poetry Review*
   "In the Beginning"
   "My Father's Hands"
   "How many miles to Babylon?"
   "I wish Wislawa Szymborska could edit my poems"
   "Akhmatova in Paris with Modigliani"

The following poems appeared in the *Veritas Review Issue IV*
   "Chess"
   "Bird Dream"
   "Hush Puppy"
   "What You Left Behind"
   "Into the Heart of the Dust"

"Dog and Bed" first appeared in the *Somerville Times* (January 25, 2023)

"In My Church, Mary Wears Red" first appeared in the *Mom Egg Review* Vol. 21

"Shakmati" first appeared in *@poetry2go*

"We Started Out as Liars" first appeared in the *Lily Poetry Review,* Issue 6, Summer 2021

"Mother to Remember" first appeared in the *Mom Egg Review,* September 2021

"The Tricorne Hat Lady" first appeared in the *Boston Literary Magazine,* February 2020

About the author

Author photo by Feda Eid

Anne Elezabeth Pluto grew up in Brooklyn, NY before it was
cool. She is Professor of Literature and Theatre at Lesley University
in Cambridge, MA where she is the artistic director of the Oxford
Street Players. She is an alumna of Shakespeare & Company and
was a member of the Worcester Shakespeare Company 2011 – 2016.
She was a member of the Boston small press scene in the late 1980s
and is one of the founders and editors at Nixes Mate Review and
Nixes Mate Books. Her publications include chapbooks: *The Frog
Princess*, White Pine Press (1985), eBook *Lubbock Electric*, Argotist
ebooks (2012), *Benign Protection* Cervena Barva Press (2016), the
edited print edition of *Lubbock Electric* Nixes Mate Books (2018),
and full-length collection *The Deepest Part of Dark*, Unlikely Stories
Press, NOLA (2020).

www.ingramcontent.com/pod-product-compliance
Lightning Source LLC
Chambersburg PA
CBHW031252120626
46545CB00007B/2779